Steadfast

Cultivating a Heart Like Mary

A Flourish Bible Study Journal

By
Mindy Kiker and Jenny Kochert

Welcome,

We're delighted that you're here. Your presence with us signals a season of refreshing, a time to dig into the Bible and hear God speak.

You hold in your hands a **Flourish Bible Study Journal** which guides you to spend time in the Word, filling your mind and heart with His truth. When you discover that He is good and that you are called, you can walk fearlessly into the future.

We have prayed that you would become *"like an olive tree flourishing in the house of God . . . trusting in God's unfailing love for ever and ever." Psalm 52:8 (NIV)*

Whatever the circumstances of your life right now, God's Word is waiting to meet you exactly where you are with the help that you need to take the next step.

We all have seasons where we drift away from Jesus and His Word. It is easy to get busy with the daily cares of life or to become embroiled in a fiery trial. This Bible Study Journal invites you to create a quiet space to cultivate confidence in your life right now. We pray that as you posture yourself to hear, you will receive the Word that you need to step forward into the fulfillment of the promises that God has spoken.

You are going to be amazed at what you discover as you pursue the daily practices of the DECLARE Bible Study Approach. One friend likens it to *"Holy Spirit sunglasses"* that allow you to see through the surface into the deep waters: *"I've been able to see deeper into the Bible than I've ever done before. The Holy Spirit has used DECLARE to bring much more life into my Bible time."* With regular use, it will become your own personal method to dig into any part of the Bible with an expectation of opening the Word and hearing Jesus speak.

This **Flourish Bible Study Journal** has been created from our God-breathed desire to walk with you, to take the truth you explore in Scripture and see it activated in your life. Regular time with Jesus nourishes the seeds of hope with the soil of truth, the sunshine of companionship, and the water of prayer to ignite growth in your heart.

May the seeds planted in your life grow and bloom as you open the Bible and enjoy time in God's presence. We stand with you in expectation at how Jesus is going to show up in your life as you feast on His Word.

Mindy & Jenny

How to get the most out of a Flourish Bible Study Journal

Like most things in life, you get out what you put into it. Go the gym and watch others do the heavy lifting, and not much is going to happen to your muscles -- but grab a set of dumbbells, start reaching for the sky, and you'll see results! Choosing a Flourish Bible Study Journal is a great first step to strengthening your spiritual muscles. And now for some hot tips on how to start reaching for the sky:

1. **Fight for your fifteen**. Set aside at least 15 minutes each day to dig in. *"Commit to the Lord whatever you do, and he will establish your plans." Proverbs 16:3 (NIV)* Five days each week, you'll work through a stage of the DECLARE Bible Study Approach focusing on the declaration scripture for that week. If you have more time, there are additional ideas for digging into the Word further. There is also an optional daily reading plan. We have designed the study with our less-is-more approach to Bible study which goes deep into a small portion of scripture using all our senses to explore God's Word.

2. **Get curious about the Word**. What does the Word say about your situation? What does it say about God himself? What does it say about your family? What does it say about the future? As you learn more about the Bible, how to study it, and how to dig deeper, you will become hungry to get into the Bible and to know it well.

3. **Get to Know Jesus**. Jesus is the Word personified. He embodies everything God desires to reveal to us. John tells us that *"the Word became flesh and dwelt among us." John 1:14 (ESV)* That's Jesus! His life of love and obedience crushed the power of death. By getting to know Him, we come to understand the whole Bible in terms of God's plan to rescue all of humanity – this includes you and me, right here, right now, today!

4. **Seek for a personal word**. When trying to gain understanding, we look for answers in several places. You may seek counsel with trusted leaders in your life. It is good to seek wisdom in a multitude of counsel, but then you must draw away to a quiet place and seek God yourself. We usually say, "Father, I have sought much advice, and now I want to know what You have to say about this situation." When we pursue God in this way, and the inevitable storms come, the Word God has spoken will hold us like an anchor to the Rock.

This is how you can flourish in faith, family and life. You dig into the Word. You fasten your gaze on the person of Jesus. You wait until you receive a personal word. The **DECLARE Bible Study Approach** is the key to bringing all these elements together. This less-is-more approach guides you to dig into the Bible and hear Jesus speak.

When we press into God's Word and hear His voice, we gain confidence that He will never fail us. God may be later than expected. He may not answer like we imagined, but He knows what we need. One of the characteristics of God is that He loves multiplication. This is good news! **When pursuing God, you get out MORE than you put into it.** *Psalm 34:4 says,* "G*od met me more than halfway."* (MSG) We're thrilled that you're here, digging in with us.

Table of Contents

Welcome 1

Reading Plan 5

DECLARE Bible Study Approach 7

Let's Walk with Mary 10

Week One: I am a Servant 13

    Devotional 14

    DECLARE 17

    Week One Discussion Topics 35

Week Two: She Who Believed 39

    Devotional 40

    DECLARE 43

    Week Two Discussion Topics 61

Week Three: Call Me Blessed 65

    Devotional 66

    DECLARE 69

    Week Three Discussion Topics 87

Week Four: Treasured and Pondered 91

    Devotional 92

    DECLARE 95

    Week Four Discussion Topics 113

Next Steps 116

A Note to Group Leaders 117

About Flourish 118

About the Authors 119

Reading Plan & Weekly Scripture Declaration

Week 1: Reading Plan – Luke 1:1-38 & Matthew Chapter 1
Declaration Verse– Luke 1:38

"And Mary said, 'Behold I am the servant of the Lord; may it be to me according to your word.'" (AMP)

Week 2: Reading Plan – Luke 1:39-45 & Mark 1:1-20
Declaration Verse – Luke 1:45

"And blessed is she who believed that there would be a fulfillment of what was spoken to her from the Lord." (ESV)

Week 3: Reading Plan – Luke 1:46-80 & John 1:1-28
Declaration Verse – Luke 1:47-49

"And my spirit rejoices in God my savior, for he has looked on the humble estate of his servant. For behold, from now on all generations will call me blessed; for he who is might has done great things for me, and holy is his name." (ESV)

Week 4: Reading Plan – Luke 2:1-20 & Galatians 4:4-7
Declaration Verse – Luke 2:19

"But Mary treasured up all these things and pondered them in her heart." (NIV)

Declare Bible Study Approach

"We know that the Son of God has come and has given us understanding, so that we may know him who is true......."

1 John 5:20

The Declare Bible Study Approach equips us to dig deeper into a passage of scripture in order to know God's Word intimately and apply it to our lives. *(1 Corinthians 2:10-15)* When His Word is activated in our midst, new life is released, and we will begin to flourish where we are planted.

Learn more about the DECLARE Bible Study Approach and how to use online Bible study aids. Log onto **www.flourishgathering.com/declare** to view our video series.

Preparation: Engage

Whenever you have time to dig into the Word, it is important to engage by tuning your ears and heart to God's voice. Take just a few minutes to pray through the following items:

Toss: Throw your cares on God. Let Him bear your burdens. *Psalm 55:22*

Catch: Receive the peace that surpasses all understanding. *Philippians 4:7*

Invite: Take every thought captive. Invite clarity and focus. Refuse confusion, distraction, or double-mindedness. *2 Corinthians 10:5*

Open: Ask God if you have turned away or closed your heart to anyone. Release the offense, open your heart, and give the situation into God's care. *Psalm 139:23*

Expect: Tell God that you are looking forward to hearing from Him. Let the excitement of time in His presence build expectation in your heart. *Habakkuk 2:1*

Stage 1: Read & Write

Start with a verse or short passage that you want to explore further:

- Read the scripture slowly once or twice, even out loud if you are able.
- Write the scripture in your journal, including verses before and after.
- Read the entire chapter for context.
- Read the passage in another translation.

Stage 2: Investigate

Once you have read the scripture and corresponding chapter, there are several options that you can use to look deeper into the meditation Scripture. Investigate as little or as much as time allows. Online resources like BibleGateway.com or BlueLetterBible.org will help:

- Highlight the words in the declaration verse you want to research more. We teach you how to do a word study to gain greater insight into the passage.
- Read other verses with a similar message, called cross references. Reading cross references will help you better understand a verse, word, or principle.
- Read a commentary.

Stage 3: Imagine

Read the meditation verse and insert yourself in the story. Use your imagination to be present in the scene. Ask yourself the following questions:

- When and where is this taking place?
- Who is speaking? About what? Why?
- What character traits of God are revealed in this scripture or chapter?
- What promises of God are shown through this scripture or chapter?

Stage 4: Listen

Invite the Words of Scripture and the Words of God to speak personally into your mind and heart. You can ask these questions:

- How do these verses apply to me?
- Is there anything that I need to receive or surrender in my life?
- Lord, how I can apply Your Word to the frustrations, disappointments, fears, or hurts in my life?

Listening can be pursued for several days, and in fact, God will probably speak unexpectedly at random times of day or night as His revelation is released to you.

Stage 5: Declare

Write out a declaration of what you have received as you meditated on the Word. This can be a statement of God's promise to you, an affirmation of the healing that He has given you, or a proclamation of a truth that has become real to you. A declaration can include Scripture, your own words, or some of each.

Let's Walk with Mary

When we say "Yes" to God, we may have an idealized notion of what life will look like: mission and purpose, victory and blessing, power and prestige. While we do experience glorious joys as we walk with Christ, there is another reality that is harder to face. In this life we also encounter confusion and hopelessness, defeat and fear, thieving and loss. Maybe this was your story in the past, or even right now. How do we find strength in these challenging times?

In this devotional and study, we seek out the steadfast heart of Mary, mother of Jesus. Hers is a story of unwavering faith and relentless hope. In the life of Mary, we find the secrets to a heart that is pierced but not crushed. This resilient woman shows us how to find our treasure in God alone.

As we walk with Mary, we are astounded by several realizations. She is:

- Yielded -- she offers herself, even her very body, as a haven for the Messiah.

- Faithful -- hope and praise are on her lips.

- Treasured -- she has hidden the Word in her heart.

- Confident -- she is filled with the Spirit and believes God can accomplish what He says.

- Steadfast -- she is unshaken by the cares of the world.

As we immerse ourselves in Scripture and prayer and become acquainted with Mary, we grow to admire her as a young woman whose heart is fixed on God. Her ponderings are focused on God's Word, not on the many what-ifs that lurk in the shadows, taunting her to doubt, to fear, or to turn away from her calling.

Mary sees God. When we see God, everything changes. (*Psalm 63:1-3*) The brilliance of His light, love, and truth obliterates the dark shadows that provide cover for the enemy. Where can evil hide when God is present?

We begin our exploration of the story of Mary, mother of Jesus, in the book of Luke. Here we are introduced to Mary's cousin, Elizabeth, and her husband Zechariah. This elderly couple have long experienced the pain of infertility, when one day Gabriel shows up promising the faithful priest that his wife is going to conceive a son.

Gabriel's next improbable revelation is the promise of a son to an unmarried maiden. Remember that God's chosen people are ever vigilant, on the lookout for the Messiah. The Hebrew Scriptures contain prophesies about the Son of God who will arrive to rescue His people, but no one knows exactly how or when He will appear. They know the arrival will involve a virgin birth (Isaiah 7:14), but the details are still a mystery.

Mary is a poor girl from a humble family, residing in an insignificant town. Why would her life be any different from anyone else's? There is nothing about her or her family that makes her stand out in any way. Yet she certainly exceeds expectations, doesn't she? When she says "Yes," she chooses a path that changes her life and the course of history.

From an unassuming start, Mary unexpectedly becomes blessed of all women. What qualities enable her to be the chosen one? Together we seek to uncover the steadfast and confident heart that makes her a woman to emulate, a daughter to admire, a sister to love. Let us learn from her story.

Week One

I Am a Servant

DECLARATION VERSE

"And Mary said, 'Behold I am the servant of the Lord;
may it be to me according to your word.'" Luke 1:38 (AMP)

As you enter your time of Bible Study this week, take a moment to Engage by tuning your ears and heart to God's voice.

Toss: Throw your cares on God. Let Him bear your burdens. *Psalm 55:22*

Catch: Receive the peace that surpasses all understanding. *Philippians 4:7*

Invite: Take every thought captive. Invite clarity and focus. Refuse confusion, distraction, or double-mindedness. *2 Corinthians 10:5*

Open: Ask God if you have turned away or closed your heart to anyone. Release the offense, open your heart, and give the situation into God's care. *Psalm 139:23*

Expect: Tell God that you are looking forward to hearing from Him. Let the excitement of time in His presence build expectation in your heart. *Habakkuk 2:1*

I am a Servant

Who is this young woman who says "Yes" to God even though life takes her into unexpected territory? What power enables her to hold fast to God's call on her life, despite circumstances that pierce her heart? Let's take a behind-the-scenes look at one of the heroes of our faith as we discover how to cultivate a steadfast faith like Mary, the mother of Jesus.

I am astounded by the strength of character she possesses at a young age. Imagine her conversation with the angel Gabriel who arrives out of nowhere to tell her that she is going to become pregnant and bear God's Son. *What?* That ranks up there with *the most outrageous thing that happened to me today!*

When I read this gospel account of Mary's encounter with Gabriel, I put myself in Mary's shoes with some difficulty – this is a Cinderella-and-the-glass-slippers moment. As I try to squeeze my bulging foot into the dainty glass slipper, I must admit that it is not a good fit.

Here's the honest truth: **when a Word of God conflicts directly with my current circumstances, my gut reaction is to doubt God**. Of course, I have not yet encountered Gabriel -- perhaps that makes it easier to believe a Word. However, I suspect that even if I encountered a brilliant angel, I would still doubt.

Besides, Gabriel is not exactly bringing good news. Mary, a betrothed but not-yet-married young lady, has no business being pregnant. When I remember my formative years in a Bible-believing church, getting pregnant before marriage was the kiss of death. *"Anything but that,"* I perceived in the youth-group teaching, even though no one used those exact words.

Mary receives this *"good news"* with some surprise. The scriptures say that she is troubled and perplexed by mysterious message this angel brings. She asks Gabriel to explain how she can become pregnant since she is a virgin. She believes Gabriel's unbelievable explanation: *"The Holy Spirit will come on you, and the power of the*

Most High will overshadow you. So, the holy one to be born will be called the Son of God. Even Elizabeth your relative is going to have a child in her old age, and she who was said to be unable to conceive is in her sixth month. For no word from God will ever fail." Luke 1:35-38 (NIV)

Luke's retelling of this encounter between Mary and Gabriel does not specify how much time elapses between the angel's answer and Mary's response. The scriptures tell us that Mary ponders in her heart, so maybe she takes a little time to mull over this explanation. Does she wrestle with the angel's words?

We read on and find that she accepts God's call with a profound yet simple statement, *"Behold, I am the servant of the Lord; may it be done to me according to your word." Luke 1:38 (AMP)*

What powerful inner strength enables her to respond with such confidence in her God? Mary inspires me, but she also mystifies me. ***How can we cultivate a steadfast heart that enables us to step into the unknown with bold confidence?***

When God delivers a word that clashes with my expectations, I realize that I hold fast to my opinions about how life should work: I will grow up, be educated, meet a man, get married, have a successful career, buy a house and car, birth two or more healthy children, grow old with my husband, and pass peacefully in old age.

Unfortunately, our expectations are not guaranteed. Some children don't grow up. Many people do not have access to education. I have several friends who longed to be married but have not realized that dream. Financial success is hard to come by. Many marriages do not last. Good people die young.

This litany of broken dreams does not mesh with our expectations of the blessings God promises to His children. But the stories in the Bible constantly challenge our expectations.

Jesus isn't exalted to the highest place until He becomes obedient, even to the point of death (Philippians 2). The disciples deny themselves and take up their cross to follow Jesus (Matthew 16). John says that we will have trouble in this world (John 16). But wait, isn't there a second part to that verse in John 16? Yes, there is it: *"But take heart! I have overcome the world." John 16:33 (NIV)*

Mary knows deep in her heart that life is gained by losing it. ***God has overcome the world, yet His overcoming power shows up in her life to the same degree that she yields her will to Him.*** We have a free will, and God does not overpower us with His invitation to follow Him. He invites us to lay down our lives, to give up our rights and our plans; however, the choice is ours. Jesus offers tough truth to his disciples, *"For whoever would save his life will lose it, but whoever loses his life for my sake will find it." Matthew 16:25 (ESV)*

This is pure gospel grit, and it comes with a question: what needs to give way in your heart for you to willingly lose your life for the sake of Christ? As we ponder these life-altering questions, Mary becomes more impressive by the minute.

I am a Servant: Day One

Declaration Verse:

"And Mary said, 'Behold I am the servant of the Lord;
may it be to me according to your word.'" Luke 1:38 (AMP)

Today's Declare Practice: Read & Write

[ ] Read Luke 1:38 slowly once or twice, even out loud if you are able.

[ ] Write Luke 1:38 in the space below. *Feel free to get creative!*

Have a little more time?

[ ] Read Luke 1:1-38 for context. Write out a few observations.

[ ] Read Luke 1:38 in another Bible translation. Do you notice any differences?

Write your observations.

Digging Deeper
Matthew Chapter 1

[ ] Read and Write

    Write any verses that stand out to you as you read Matthew Chapter 1.

[ ] Write down any general thoughts or questions you have as you read the verses today.

I am a Servant: Day Two

Declaration Verse: Luke 1:38

Today's Declare Practice: Investigate

Today we begin looking deeper into the Declaration Verse. Investigate as little or as much as time allows. Online resources like BibleGateway.com or BlueLetterBible.org will help you during your investigation.

[ ] Conduct a Word Study: Part One

Read the Declaration Verse and Luke 1:1-38. Spend a few minutes highlighting any words you want to research more.

Write these words below.

[ ] Conduct a Word Study: Part Two

Want to learn more about the DECLARE Bible Study Approach and how to do a word study? Log onto **www.flourishgathering.com/declare** to view our video series.

Using BlueLetterBible.org or another online resource, choose a word you selected above to conduct your word study. This is as simple as looking up the original Greek or Hebrew word, reading the definitions of that word, and looking at how it is used in other verses in the Bible.

Record the results of your word study here.

Have a little more time?

[ ] Read any of the following cross references for Luke 1:38:

    2 Samuel 7:25-29
    Psalm 116:16
    Romans 4:20-21

Reading cross references will help you better understand a verse, word, or principle.

What did you discover? Write your insights.

[ ] Read a commentary. A commentary is a collection of explanatory notes that a Bible scholar has written about scripture. You can find these online. A good place to begin is Matthew Henry, C.H. Spurgeon, or David Guzik. Write any observations, quotes, or notes.

Digging Deeper
Matthew Chapter 1

[ ] Investigate

Highlight a couple of key words that stand out to you in Matthew Chapter 1. Using BlueLetterBible.org, look up the Greek or Hebrew word and definition of one of those words.

Write your findings below.

[ ] Write down any general thoughts or questions you have as you read the chapter.

I am a Servant: Day Three

Declaration Verse: Luke 1:38

Today's Declare Practice: Imagine

> *Remember to take a moment to Engage as you prepare to listen: toss, catch, invite, open, expect. Invite the Words of Scripture and the Words of God to speak personally into your mind and heart.*

[ ] Read Luke 1:38

You may want to scout around in your Bible for any notes or perhaps an introduction to this book of the Bible. When using your imagination, it helps to keep in mind the context of the chapter and book that you're in. Insert yourself in the story as you ponder the following questions. Use your imagination and all your senses to be present in the scene.

[ ] When and where is this taking place? What do you imagine you might see, hear, touch, taste, or smell?

[ ] Who is speaking or writing? Who are they addressing? Others? God? Themselves?

[ ] What are they speaking or writing about? What is their purpose?

Have a little more time?

[ ] What are the character traits of God as shown through the Declaration Verse?

   Is He steadfast, faithful, just, trustworthy, nurturing, kind, gentle, or strong?
   What do you see revealed about His nature in this passage of Scripture?

[ ] What are the promises of God as shown through the Declaration Verse?

   Write any observations, key words, or questions you have as you ponder the
   Declaration Verse. If you have time, you may want to do another word study.

Digging Deeper
Matthew Chapter 1

[ ] Imagine

    Compare the stories told in Luke 1 and Matthew 1.

    What is happening? What do you notice? Anything surprising?

[ ] Write down any general thoughts or questions you have as you read the chapter today. Note the differences between the Luke and Matthew accounts.

I am a Servant: Day Four

Declaration Verse: Luke 1:38

Today's Declare Practice: Listen

> *Remember to take a moment to Engage as you prepare to listen: toss, catch, invite, open, expect. Invite the Words of Scripture and the Words of God to speak personally into your mind and heart. Remember that God's voice will never accuse you. He may bring gentle conviction, and that can cause some grief, but God always brings hope.*

Listening can be pursued for several days, and in fact, God will probably speak unexpectedly at random times of day or night as His revelation is released to you. Ask these questions as you listen to God's voice.

[ ] How does this verse apply to me?

Have a little more time?

[ ] Ponder and pray: how I can apply these truths to the frustrations, disappointments, fears, or hurts in my life? Is there anything I need to surrender or receive in my life?

Digging Deeper
Matthew Chapter 1

[ ] Listen

Ask yourself: how does the reading in Luke and Matthew apply to me?
What does God want to speak to my heart through these verses?

[ ] Write down any general thoughts or questions you have as you ponder
   the passages.

I am a Servant: Day Five

Declaration Verse: Luke 1:38

Today's Declare Practice: Declare

Write out a declaration of what you have received as you meditated on the Word. This can be a statement of God's promise to you, an affirmation of the healing that He has given you, or a proclamation of a truth that has become real to you. A declaration can include Scripture, your own words, or some of each.

Reflect upon your week

Write out Luke 1:38 by hand if you memorized it or summarize the Declaration Verse in your own words below.

Spend a few minutes documenting your insights, "a-ha" moments, and revelations from this week of digging into the Bible.

Digging Deeper
Matthew Chapter 1

[ ] Write any notes or observations you made from reading the passage.
    Is there one verse that stands out to you?

[ ] Record one new insight that came as you pondered the verses in Luke & Matthew.

Week One: Discussion Topics

Use these discussion topics to gather with friends and enjoy this study together. You are welcome to use these points to help guide your conversation, or you can ponder these questions as a personal reflection. Even if you are not able to meet up with a girlfriend, you're invited to join us in our private Facebook Group at facebook.com/groups/flourishgathering/

1) Do you have any thoughts or reactions to this week's devotional? We have included two passages that may inspire an interesting conversation:

"Here's the honest truth: **when a Word of God conflicts directly with my current circumstances, my gut reaction is to doubt God.** *Of course, I have not yet encountered Gabriel -- perhaps that makes it easier to believe a Word. However, I suspect that even if I encountered a brilliant angel, I would still doubt ."* (page 12)

"Mary knows deep in her heart that life is gained by losing it. **God has overcome the world, yet His overcoming power shows up in her life to the same degree that she yields her will to Him.** *We have a free will, and God does not overpower us with His invitation to follow Him. He invites us to lay down our lives, to give up our rights and our plans; however, the choice is ours."* (page 14)

2) Was there a special insight you gained from the **Investigate** practice? Perhaps an interesting word study, cross reference, or commentary?

3) What happened when you used your **Imagination**? What did you discover about the context of this chapter or book of the Bible? If you had time, did you gain insight into the character or promises of God?

4) Did God speak something special that you would like to share as you **Listened**?
5) What is your **Declaration**? How can we pray for you in this regard?
6) How about the Ruth reading plan? Anything interesting there?
7) How can we support one another this week? Prayer requests? Praise reports?

Notes

Notes

Week Two

She Who Believed

DECLARATION VERSE

"And blessed is she who believed that there would be a fulfillment of what was spoken to her from the Lord." Luke 1:45 (ESV)

As you enter your time of Bible Study this week, take a moment to Engage by tuning your ears and heart to God's voice.

Toss: Throw your cares on God. Let Him bear your burdens. *Psalm 55:22*

Catch: Receive the peace that surpasses all understanding. *Philippians 4:7*

Invite: Take every thought captive. Invite clarity and focus. Refuse confusion, distraction, or double-mindedness. *2 Corinthians 10:5*

Open: Ask God if you have turned away or closed your heart to anyone. Release the offense, open your heart, and give the situation into God's care. *Psalm 139:23*

Expect: Tell God that you are looking forward to hearing from Him. Let the excitement of time in His presence build expectation in your heart. *Habakkuk 2:1*

She Who Believed

Before we leave the scene unfolding in Luke chapter one and move on in the story, let's sit here a little while longer and ponder the magnitude of this encounter with the angel Gabriel. As I read the words of Gabriel, I come to a screeching halt right here:

"*And behold* [as in FYI or P.P.S.] *your relative Elizabeth in her old age* [are you catching the details?] *has also conceived a son, and this is the sixth month with her who was called barren.*" (Luke 1:36)

This is significant! Not only for Mary, as we will come to find out, yet also for you and me.

God gives Mary some heavy information, but He doesn't leave her hanging, wondering once the angel leaves if she heard correctly or if it were a dream -- or worse, was she going mad?

Would anyone believe this story? Would Joseph think she was playing childish games?

God knows that Mary needs to see a miracle unfolding. The angel Gabriel tells of the miracle child in Elizabeth's womb, to be named John, just as the miracle begins coming to life in Mary's body.

Before this servant of God utters her famous last words to Gabriel, he says, *"For nothing will be impossible with God." (Luke 1:37)*

I'm sure the gossip mill was busy over the decades that Elizabeth was barren. As Elizabeth aged, her chances of becoming pregnant were slim, and now at her old age (Gabriel's words, not mine), they were non-existent. Mary would have grown up overhearing the family drama of Elizabeth's shameful circumstances.

The words Gabriel speaks become her first life-line as this story plays out. Seemingly insignificant details viewed in light of the greater story reveal her foundation of faith, the building of her steadfast heart.

Sometimes the revelation we've just been hit with feels as if we have been left stranded without a life preserver. We feel we are wading through the sea of despair, waiting for the promise to be fulfilled. Yet, I believe that God always reveals a life-line, even though *we don't always see it right away.*

Several years ago, I walked hand in hand alongside a dear friend who lost her three-year old son to a brain injury. It was one of the most heart-wrenching and emotionally exhausting moments of my life.

Watching a mother lose a child is not for the faint of heart. I drove home the night he passed away, and my mouth could utter only one refrain through tear-stained sobs: "OH, GOD, that was more painful than anyone should ever endure!"

I got home and cried myself to sleep with the grief of the night pressed on my chest. The next morning, I began processing the events with God because in my spirit I knew something was wrong within me.

I then heard Holy Spirit ask me, *"Jenny, what did you pray for?"*

"Well, I prayed for peace, strength, your presence, and something about it being beautiful in the midst of suffering."

At that moment He took me back to the night before, in my mind's eye, and said: "Didn't you see My strength in a mother holding her dying child? Didn't you see My peace poured out as everyone sang worship songs and praised My name?" God showed me He was there all along -- our life-line, our comforter.

This is what happens in the storms in our life. The overwhelming reality of the natural overwhelms us and *we lose our focus and start staring at the problem, losing sight of the promise.*

Let's get back to the story of Mary. Luke 1:39 shows Mary going with haste to visit her relative Elizabeth. Don't you love the details? She didn't just go see Elizabeth -- she went with a fire in her belly.

When she arrives, well, there is quite a scene filled with leaping babies, the presence of the Holy Spirit, and loud exclamations.

Before we leave this glorious scene, Elizabeth utters powerful words that give us a glimpse into the heart of Mary:

"And blessed is she who believed that there would be a fulfillment of what was spoken to her from the Lord." Luke 1:45

As if this story can't get any better! When I ponder these words, I am reminded of 2 Corinthians 5:7 which tells us to walk by faith and not by sight. I realize that I had something backward all this time. This scripture doesn't imply that we don't need our sight. Instead, it tells us that faith must come first.

When Elizabeth utters those affirming words to Mary, she confirms that Mary believes that which could not yet be seen. However, God knows she will also need to see Elizabeth's bulging six-month belly to remind her that nothing is impossible with God and that the promise spoken to her would be fulfilled.

This is where I believe a steadfast and confident heart comes from. When we see obstacles, we ask God, *"Please show me your hand."* He shows Mary a bulging, leaping belly, and her faith is bolstered. God is good, and He longs for us to see His glory, to perceive His outstretched hand in the chaos in our lives, our families, and our hurting world. I want to be like Mary, running with haste to see the hand of God.

Ladies, our stories aren't easy, the roads we travel are often broken and our hearts long for the promise fulfilled. Yet, sometimes in the midst of the suffering, the waiting, the unknown, we must choose to see--and we must choose to believe.

She Who Believed: Day One

Declaration Verse:

"And blessed is she who believed that there would be a fulfillment of what was spoken to her from the Lord." Luke 1:45 (ESV)

Today's Declare Practice: Read & Write

[ ] Read Luke 1:45 slowly once or twice, even out loud if you are able.

[ ] Write Luke 1:45 in the space below. *Feel free to get creative!*

Have a little more time?

[ ] Read Luke 1:39-45 for context. Write out a few observations.

[ ] Read Luke 1:45 in another Bible translation. Do you notice any differences?

Write your observations.

Digging Deeper
Mark 1:1-20

[ ] Read Mark 1:1-20

[ ] Read and Write

Write any verses that stand out to you as you read the verses.

[ ] Write down any general thoughts or questions you as you read the
passage.

She Who Believed: Day Two

Declaration Verse: Luke 1:45

Today's Declare Practice: Investigate

Today we begin looking deeper into the Declaration Verse. Investigate as little or as much as time allows. Online resources like BibleGateway.com or BlueLetterBible.org will help you during your investigation.

[ ] Conduct a Word Study: Part One

Read the Declaration Verse. Spend a few minutes highlighting any words you want to research more.

Write these words below.

[ ] Conduct a Word Study: Part Two

Want to learn more about the DECLARE Bible Study Approach and how to do a word study? Log onto **www.flourishgathering.com/declare** to view our video series.

Using BlueLetterBible.org or another online resource, choose a word you selected above to conduct your word study. This is as simple as looking up the original Greek or Hebrew word, reading the definitions of that word, and looking at how it is used in other verses in the Bible.

Record the results of your word study here.

Have a little more time?

[ ] Read any of the following cross references for Luke 1:45:

Jeremiah 17:7-8
Psalm 34:8
2 Corinthians 1:20

Reading cross references will help you better understand a verse, word, or principle.

What did you discover? Write your insights:

[ ] Read a commentary. A commentary is a collection of explanatory notes that a Bible scholar has written about scripture. You can find these online. A good place to begin is Matthew Henry, C.H. Spurgeon, or David Guzik. Write any observations, quotes, or notes.

Digging Deeper
Mark 1:1-20

[ ] Investigate

Highlight a couple of key words that stand out to you in the verses you read. Using BlueLetterBible.org look up the Greek or Hebrew word and definition of one of those words.

Write your findings below.

[ ] Write down any general thoughts or questions you have as you read the passage today.

She Who Believed: Day Three

Declaration Verse: Luke 1:45

Today's Declare Practice: Imagine

Remember to take a moment to Engage as you prepare to listen: toss, catch, invite, open, expect. Invite the Words of Scripture and the Words of God to speak personally into your mind and heart.

[ ] Read Luke 1:45

Insert yourself in the story as you ponder the following questions. Use your imagination and all your senses to be present in the scene.

[ ] When and where is this taking place? What do you imagine you might see, hear, touch, taste, or smell?

[ ] Who is speaking or writing? Who are they addressing? Others? God? Themselves?

[ ] What are they speaking or writing about? What is their purpose?

Have a little more time?

[ ] What character traits of God are revealed through the Declaration Verse?

Is He steadfast, faithful, just, trustworthy, nurturing, kind, gentle, or strong?
What do you see revealed about His nature in this passage of Scripture?

[ ] What are the promises of God as shown through the Declaration Verse?

Write any observations, key words, or questions you have as you ponder the
Declaration Verse. If you have time, you may want to do another word study.

Digging Deeper
Mark 1:1-20

[ ] Imagine

    Compare the stories told in Luke 1 and Mark 1.

    What is happening? What do you notice? Anything surprising?

[ ] Write down any general thoughts or questions you have as you read the passage. Note the differences between the Luke and Mark accounts.

She Who Believed: Day Four

Declaration Verse: Luke 1:45

Today's Declare Practice: Listen

Remember to take a moment to Engage as you prepare to listen: toss, catch, invite, open, expect. Invite the Words of Scripture and the Words of God to speak personally into your mind and heart. Remember that God's voice will never accuse you. He may bring gentle conviction, and that can cause some grief, but God always brings hope.

Listening can be pursued for several days, and in fact, God will probably speak unexpectedly at random times of day or night as His revelation is released to you. Ask these questions as you listen to God's voice:

[ ] How does this verse apply to me?

Have a little more time?

[ ] Ponder and pray: how I can apply these truths to the frustrations,
   disappointments, fears, or hurts in my life? Is there anything I need to receive
   or surrender in my life?

Digging Deeper
Mark 1:1-20

[ ] Listen

Ask yourself: how do the truths in Mark 1:1-20 apply to me? How does God want to speak to my heart through this story?

[ ] Write down any general thoughts or questions you have as you ponder the verses.

She Who Believed: Day Five

Declaration Verse: Luke 1:45

Today's Declare Practice: Declare

Write out a declaration of what you have received as you meditated on the Word. This can be a statement of God's promise to you, an affirmation of the healing that He has given you, or a proclamation of a truth that has become real to you. A declaration can include Scripture, your own words, or some of each.

Reflect upon your week

Write out Luke 1:45 by hand if you memorized it or summarize the Declaration Verse in your own words below.

Spend a few minutes documenting your insights, "a-ha" moments, and revelations from this week of digging into the Bible.

Digging Deeper
Mark 1:1-20

[ ] Write any notes or observations you made from the verses.
    Is there one verse that stands out to you?

[ ] Did you have any new insights as you pondered Mark this week?

Week Two: Discussion Topics

Use these discussion topics to gather with friends and enjoy this study together. You are welcome to use these points to help guide your conversation, or you can ponder these questions as a personal reflection. Even if you are not able to meet up with a girlfriend, you're invited to join us in our private Facebook Group at facebook.com/groups/flourishgathering/

1) Do you have any thoughts or reactions to this week's devotional? We have included two passages that may inspire an interesting conversation:

> "Sometimes the revelation we've just been hit with feels as if we have been left stranded without a life preserver. We feel we are wading through the sea of despair, waiting for the promise to be fulfilled. Yet, I believe that God always reveals a life-line, even though *we don't always see it right away*." (page 37)

> "As if this story can't get any better! When I ponder these words [in Luke 1:45], I am reminded of 2 Corinthians 5:7 which tells us to walk by faith and not by sight. I realize that I had something backward all this time. This scripture doesn't imply that we don't need our sight. Instead, it tells us that faith must come first." (page 38)

2) Was there a special insight you gained from the **Investigate** practice? Perhaps an interesting word study, cross reference, or commentary?

3) What happened when you used your **Imagination**? What did you discover about the context of this chapter or book of the Bible? If you had time, did you gain insight into the character or promises of God?

4) Did God speak something special that you would like to share as you **Listened**?
5) What is your **Declaration**? How can we pray for you in this regard?
6) How about the Ruth reading plan? Anything interesting there?
7) How can we support one another this week? Prayer requests? Praise reports?

Notes

Notes

Week Three

Call Me Blessed

DECLARATION VERSE

"And my spirit rejoices in God my savior, for he has looked on the humble estate of his servant. For behold, from now on all generations will call me blessed; for he who is mighty has done great things for me, and holy is his name."
Luke 1:47-49 (ESV)

As you enter your time of Bible Study this week, take a moment to Engage by tuning your ears and heart to God's voice.

Toss: Throw your cares on God. Let Him bear your burdens. *Psalm 55:22*
Catch: Receive the peace that surpasses all understanding. *Philippians 4:7*
Invite: Take every thought captive. Invite clarity and focus. Refuse confusion, distraction, or double-mindedness. *2 Corinthians 10:5*
Open: Ask God if you have turned away or closed your heart to anyone. Release the offense, open your heart, and give the situation into God's care. *Psalm 139:23*
Expect: Tell God that you are looking forward to hearing from Him. Let the excitement of time in His presence build expectation in your heart. *Habakkuk 2:1*

Call Me Blessed

After Mary encounters Gabriel, she decides to make the trek seventy or eighty miles south to her cousin's house in Judea. Most historians believe the journey took her three or four days. Mary is accustomed to walking long distances, though her state of mind is revealed in that she embarks *"with haste."*

What is Mary running from? Or running to?

You see, Mary is in a cultural pickle. Although I believe Mary fully trusts God, she is fourteen, unmarried, and just found out that she is going to birth the Savior of the world!

In modern talk, you might say that Gabriel just *"dropped the mic"* on her.

Why does the angel also include specific information about Mary's cousin who is also pregnant? This news surely encourages Mary who knows this is a miraculous pregnancy for Elizabeth and Zacharias.

Are you catching the significance of the timing? *Coincidence? I think not!*

Mary sets out to see Elizabeth *"with haste."* Of course, she does. If she stayed in Nazareth, Mary would have been signing up for self-imposed isolation at best -- or worst, social ostracism -- a potential threat in her hometown.

I imagine that Mary didn't want to be alone. I wouldn't want to be alone in those circumstances. **In His kindness, God provides companionship for His daughter.**

When we find ourselves in hard seasons of our own, author Sophie Hudson expresses God's care in companionship. I couldn't agree with her more:

"When the Holy Spirit in one woman recognizes and responds to the Holy Spirit in another woman, safe places become sacred places." (Hudson, Giddy up, Eunice)

Watch as Mary's safe place with Elizabeth becomes a sacred place! After her long journey, Mary, finds instant understanding and a loud cry of excitement from her cousin. What a relief this joyous reception must have been!

Matthew Henry gives us insight into this special moment:

"It does not appear that Elizabeth had been told anything of her cousin Mary's being designed for the mother of the Messiah; and therefore, what knowledge she appears to have had of it must have come by a revelation, which would be a great encouragement to Mary." (Commentary, Luke 1:39-56)

What I love about real, honest and genuine relationships between women is that we find comfort and encouragement from someone in similar circumstances. Mary and Elizabeth both find themselves in situations they never could have imagined.

This is where women thrive best: in the molding and meshing of similar seasons and stories. **We are simply better walking through life together.**

Within the first few moments of their greeting, Elizabeth, encourages, affirms, tends, and blesses Mary. And it draws from Mary a eloquent response forever marked in history.

At this point in the story, we haven't heard much from Mary. Except for an honest question to the angel Gabriel, asking him to clarify how she could possibly become pregnant, being a virgin and all. Except for this query and a profound statement agreeing to go along with the plan, Mary has been quiet on the scene.

Yet, after Elizabeth affirms and encourages Mary, Mary belts out a song of praise that leaves me speechless:

"And Mary said, my soul magnifies the Lord, and my spirit rejoices in God my Savior, for he has looked on the humble estate of his servant. For behold, from now on all generations will call me blessed; for he who is mighty has done great things for me, and holy is his name" Luke 1:46-49

I don't know about you, but I had to read her song of praise several dozen times to grasp the magnitude of her words. Mary's faith is on fire and in large part because of Elizabeth.

That is what we as the body of Christ can do for one other: *to stir up each other's faith to believe, to affirm our sister's calling, to encourage a friend's soul, to bear one other's burdens!*

Sisters in Christ, **we have the power to be the Elizabeth's to the Mary's of this world.** We can be the friend who sees with spiritual eyes that God is at work deep inside another, and we can speak hope into the mysteries, confidence into the uncertainties.

Just when a sister is in distress, our words empowered by God may infuse her whole being with faith and endurance.

Let us rise up to encourage and affirm each other because we never know the true weight of the calling that a sister may be carrying. When we offer the life-giving words of Elizabeth to another, we may be offering her the strength she needs to bring forth what God has called her to birth. How this companionship will bless and affirm our soul as well!

Call Me Blessed: Day One

Declaration Verse:

"And my spirit rejoices in God my savior, for he has looked on the humble estate of his servant. For behold, from now on all generations will call me blessed; for he who is mighty has done great things for me, and holy is his name." Luke 1:47-49 (ESV)

Today's Declare Practice: Read & Write

[ ] Read Luke 1:47-49 slowly once or twice, even out loud if you are able.

[ ] Write Luke 1:47-49 in the space below. *Feel free to get creative!*

Have a little more time?

[ ] Read Luke 1:46-80 for context. Write out a few observations.

[ ] Read Luke 1:47-49 in another Bible translation. Do you notice any differences?

Write your observations.

Digging Deeper
John 1:1-28

[ ] Read John 1:1-28

[ ] Read and Write

    Write any verses that stand out to you as you read the verses.

[ ] Write down any general thoughts or questions you have as you read the passage.

Call Me Blessed: Day Two

Declaration Verse: Luke 1:47-49

Today's Declare Practice: Investigate

Today we begin looking deeper into the Declaration Verse. Investigate as little or as much as time allows. Online resources like BibleGateway.com or BlueLetterBible.org will help you during your investigation.

[ ] Conduct a Word Study: Part One

Read the Declaration Verse. Spend a few minutes highlighting any words you want to research more.

Write these words below.

[ ] Conduct a Word Study: Part Two

Want to learn more about the DECLARE Bible Study Approach and how to do a word study? Log onto **www.flourishgathering.com/declare** to view our video series.

Using BlueLetterBible.org or another online resource, choose a word you selected above to conduct your word study. This is as simple as looking up the original Greek or Hebrew word, reading the definitions of that word, and looking at how it is used in other verses in the Bible.

Record the results of your word study here:

Have a little more time?

[ ] Read any of the following cross references for Luke 1:47-49:

   Psalm 35:9
   Isaiah 12:2-3
   1 Samuel 2:1-2

Reading cross references will help you better understand a verse, word, or principle.

What did you discover? Write your insights.

[ ] Read a commentary. A commentary is a collection of explanatory notes that a Bible scholar has written about scripture. You can find these online. A good place to begin is Matthew Henry, C.H. Spurgeon, or David Guzik. Write any observations, quotes, or notes.

Digging Deeper
John 1:1-28

[ ] Read John 1:1-28

[ ] Investigate

    Highlight a couple of key words that stand out to you in the verses you read. Using BlueLetterBible.org look up the Greek or Hebrew word and definition of one of those words.

    Write your findings below.

[ ] Write down any general thoughts or questions you have as you read the passage.

Call Me Blessed: Day Three

Declaration Verse: Luke 1:47-49

Today's Declare Practice: Imagine

Remember to take a moment to Engage as you prepare to listen: toss, catch, invite, open, expect. Invite the Words of Scripture and the Words of God to speak personally into your mind and heart.

[ ] Read Luke 1:47-49

Insert yourself in the story as you ponder the following questions. Use your imagination and all your senses to be present in the scene.

[ ] When and where is this taking place? **What do you imagine you might see, hear, touch, taste, or smell?**

[ ] Who is speaking or writing? Who are they addressing? Others? God?
    Themselves?

[ ] What are they speaking or writing about? What is their purpose?

Have a little more time?

[ ] What is the character of God as shown through the Declaration Verse?

Is He steadfast, faithful, just, trustworthy, nurturing, kind, gentle, or strong? What do you see revealed about His nature in this passage of Scripture?

[ ] What are the promises of God as shown through the Declaration Verse?

Write any observations, key words, or questions you have as you ponder the Declaration Verse. If you have time, you may want to do another word study.

Digging Deeper
John 1:1-28

[ ] Imagine

Compare the stories told in Luke 1 and John 1.
What is happening? What do you notice? Anything surprising?

[ ] Write down any general thoughts or questions you have as you read the verses. Note the differences between the Luke and John accounts.

Call Me Blessed: Day Four

Declaration Verse: Luke 1:47-49

Today's Declare Practice: Listen

Remember to take a moment to Engage as you prepare to listen: toss, catch, invite, open, expect. Invite the Words of Scripture and the Words of God to speak personally into your mind and heart. Remember that God's voice will never accuse you. He may bring gentle conviction, and that can cause some grief, but God always brings hope.

Listening can be pursued for several days, and in fact, God will probably speak unexpectedly at random times of day or night as His revelation is released to you. Ask these questions as you listen to God's voice:

[ ] How do these verses apply to me?

Have a little more time?

[ ] Ponder and pray: how I can apply these truths to the frustrations, disappointments, fears, or hurts in my life? Is there anything I need to receive or surrender in my life?

Digging Deeper
John 1:1-28

[ ] Listen

    Ask yourself: how do these verses in John apply to me? What does God want to speak to my heart through this passage?

[ ] Write down any general thoughts or questions you have as you ponder the verses.

Call Me Blessed: Day Five

Declaration Verse: Luke 1:47-49

Today's Declare Practice: Declare

Write out a declaration of what you have received as you meditated on the Word. This can be a statement of God's promise to you, an affirmation of the healing that He has given you, or a proclamation of a truth that has become real to you. A declaration can include Scripture, your own words, or some of each.

Reflect upon your week

Write out Luke 1:47-49 by hand if you memorized it or summarize the Declaration Verse in your own words below.

Spend a few minutes documenting your insights, "a-ha" moments, and revelations from this week of digging into the Bible.

Digging Deeper
John 1:1-28

[ ] Write any notes or observations you made from the verses you read.
    Is there one verse that stands out to you?

[ ] Did you have any new insights as you pondered the verses in John this week?

Week Three: Discussion Topics

Use these discussion topics to gather with friends and enjoy this study together. You are welcome to use these points to help guide your conversation, or you can ponder these questions as a personal reflection. Even if you are not able to meet up with a girlfriend, you're invited to join us in our private Facebook Group at facebook.com/groups/flourishgathering/

1) Do you have any thoughts or reactions to this week's devotional? We have included two passages that may inspire an interesting conversation:

> *"What I love about real, honest and genuine relationships between women is that we find comfort and encouragement from someone in similar circumstances. Mary and Elizabeth both find themselves in situations they never could have imagined. This is where women thrive best: in the molding and meshing of similar seasons and stories. **We are simply better walking through life together.**"* (page 61)

> *"Sisters in Christ, **we have the power to be the Elizabeth's to the Mary's of this world.** We can be the friend who sees with spiritual eyes that God is at work deep inside another, and we can speak hope into the mysteries, confidence into the uncertainties."* (page 62)

2) Was there a special insight you gained from the **Investigate** practice? Perhaps an interesting word study, cross reference, or commentary?

3) What happened when you used your **Imagination**? What did you discover about the context of this chapter or book of the Bible? If you had time, did you gain insight into the character or promises of God?

4) Did God speak something special that you would like to share as you **Listened**?
5) What is your **Declaration**? How can we pray for you in this regard?
6) How about the Ruth reading plan? Anything interesting there?
7) How can we support one another this week? Prayer requests? Praise reports?

Notes

Notes

Week Four

Treasured and Pondered

DECLARATION VERSE

*"Mary treasured up all these things
and pondered them in her heart." Luke 2:19*

As you enter your time of Bible Study this week, take a moment to Engage by tuning your ears and heart to God's voice.

Toss: Throw your cares on God. Let Him bear your burdens. *Psalm 55:22*

Catch: Receive the peace that surpasses all understanding. *Philippians 4:7*

Invite: Take every thought captive. Invite clarity and focus. Refuse confusion, distraction, or double-mindedness. *2 Corinthians 10:5*

Open: Ask God if you have turned away or closed your heart to anyone. Release the offense, open your heart, and give the situation into God's care. *Psalm 139:23*

Expect: Tell God that you are looking forward to hearing from Him. Let the excitement of time in His presence build expectation in your heart. *Habakkuk 2:1*

Treasured and Pondered

Mary's marvelous song of praise stirs hope in our hearts. How does she have the strength of spirit to say "yes" to God under these challenging circumstances? We discover that her **surrendered** heart enables her to yield to God when she recognizes herself as a servant and bravely agrees to mother a son in a most unusual fashion (*Luke 1:38*).

She is equally sustained by her **faithful** heart. Certain that God will fulfill His promises, she believes that God is trustworthy (*Luke 1:45-49*).

We now find Mary and Joseph heading to Bethlehem in Judea because Caesar Augustus wants to take a census of the whole Roman world. This edict brings Mary and Joseph to the place where it was prophesied that the Messiah would be born, and so He is, right there in a stable. God sends unlikely witnesses to sing the praises of the newborn King. Unsuspecting shepherds, hanging out in a field with some sheep, are urged by an angel to go find the Messiah baby who is wrapped in cloths and lying in a manger.

Watch for it – God sends another confirmation – a Word that Mary can hang onto when she is tempted to doubt or forget what God promised. First it is Elizabeth who encourages our young heroine, and now the shepherds confirm that this is no ordinary baby. All who hear are amazed, but not Mary. She had a different response:

"Mary treasured up all these things and pondered them in her heart."
(Luke 2:19)

Mary treasures God's Words to her, actively reflecting on what He has spoken to her through Gabriel and through the Holy Scriptures.

One of the definitions of the word "*treasured*" is "*to preserve a thing from perishing or being lost.*" When we fix God's words in our minds and talk about them day and night, we remind ourselves to believe. (*Deuteronomy 11:17-18*)

However, the reverse is also true. ***Without the sacred practice of treasuring and pondering, we may lose God's words.*** If we do not remember what He has done, if we forget what He has promised, those promises may perish or be lost.

However, they are not lost in God's heart. Every Word that He has ever spoken remains (*Isaiah 40:8*), but if we fail to treasure and ponder what He has said, His promises may be lost from our heart and mind.

When we fail to remember the promises, we gradually drift from His way. If our gaze is not fixed daily on God, our eyes wander to distractions, and before long we find ourselves on other paths, confused about our direction, unsure where we are on the map . . . or maybe we have lost the map altogether, and we find ourselves chasing lesser things:

"You must not turn aside, for then you would go after futile things which cannot profit or deliver, because they are futile." (1 Samuel 12:21)

Mary does not turn aside because she remembers God's promises. The very act of pondering --turning His words over and over in her mind -- keeps Mary's heart ***steadfast*** to her calling and firmly secured to God's purposes. She does not veer off course because her mind and heart continually rehearse God's Word.

What do you ponder in your heart?

I remember a time I was intensely frustrated with a family friend. As I weeded my flower bed one Sunday afternoon, I let my mind wander to rehearsing the wrong that this man had committed, how arrogant he was, how misguided.

I didn't even notice what I was treasuring in my heart – I was on auto mode, my thoughts running rampant, pondering all his wrongs. I eventually regained awareness and tapped into my heart, surprised by the cursing. As I pulled the next weed, I heard God say, *"You have some weeding to do on the inside too."*

Singing praises is not what I was doing with my thoughts that day. I was cursing, and that created a darkness of heart that brought on self-pity and hopelessness. My heart was choked with weeds. My emotions followed my thoughts down into a spiral of despair. My misguided ponderings poisoned my thoughts.

How do we pay attention to what is in our hearts? Ann Voskamp points out in her book, *1000 Gifts*, that we cannot entertain negative attitudes like spite and anger in our hearts while at the same time expressing gratitude.

We find that ***when we choose gratitude, we position our hearts toward God and displace the other attitudes that drag us down into a pit of darkness.*** That is why Mary praises God! Gratitude displaces cursing. Praise infuses our hearts with light.

I now tune in regularly to my ponderings. Like Mary, I can choose what I treasure and what thoughts I turn over and over in my mind. Mary's heart is fixed on God. Her ponderings focus on God's Word, and not on the many "what-if's" that lurk in the shadows, taunting her to doubt, to fear, or to turn away from His promises.

Spending time in God's Word, filling our minds and hearts with His truth, and praising Him with our lips equips us to respond with an unwavering *"Yes"* to God's call on our lives. When we know that He is good and that we are called, we too can walk fearlessly into the future. Stepping out faithfully when God calls us begins with the treasures of our hearts.

Growth is accomplished in our lives quietly, gradually, incrementally, in the normal stuff of daily living. Nothing spectacular. Nothing profound. Just life. With God. Except that when you look back and see all that He has accomplished, your story testifies to His redemption, His power, and His faithfulness. Let us ponder all that He has done. I encourage you to allow God to take you on a reflective journey to find the treasure in your journey. Spend time with Mary as you discover your story of "Yes."

Treasured and Pondered: Day One

Declaration Verse:

"Mary treasured up all these things and pondered them in her heart." Luke 2:19

Today's Declare Practice: Read & Write

[ ] Read Luke 2:19 slowly once or twice, even out loud if you are able.

[ ] Write Luke 2:19 in the space below. *Feel free to get creative!*

Have a little more time?

[ ] Read Luke 2:1-20 for context. Write out a few observations.

[ ] Read Luke 2:19 in another Bible translation. Do you notice any differences?

Write your observations.

Digging Deeper
Galatians 4:4-7

[ ] Read Galatians 4:4-7

[ ] Read and Write

Write any verses that stand out to you as you read the passage.

[ ] Write down any general thoughts or questions you have as you read the
verses.

Treasured and Pondered: Day Two

Declaration Verse: Luke 2:19

Today's Declare Practice: Investigate

Today we begin looking deeper into the Declaration Verse. Investigate as little or as much as time allows. Online resources like BibleGateway.com or BlueLetterBible.org will help you during your investigation.

[ ] Conduct a Word Study: Part One

Read the Declaration Verse or the entire chapter if you have more time. Spend a few minutes highlighting any words you want to research more.

Write these words below.

[ ] Conduct a Word Study: Part Two

Want to learn more about the DECLARE Bible Study Approach and how to do a word study? Log onto **www.flourishgathering.com/declare** to view our video series.

Using BlueLetterBible.org or another online resource, choose a word you selected above to conduct your word study. This is as simple as looking up the original Greek or Hebrew word, reading the definitions of that word, and looking at how it is used in other verses in the Bible.

Record the results of your word study here.

Have a little more time?

[ ] Read any of the following cross references for Luke 2:19:

Psalm 119:11
Philippians 4:8-9
Matthew 6:21

Reading cross references will help you better understand a verse, word, or principle.

What did you discover? Write your insights.

[ ] Read a commentary. A commentary is a collection of explanatory notes that a Bible scholar has written about scripture. You can find these online. A good place to begin is Matthew Henry, C.H. Spurgeon, or David Guzik. Write any observations, quotes, or notes.

Digging Deeper
Galatians 4:4-7

[ ] Investigate

Highlight a couple of key words that stand out to you in the verses you read. Using BlueLetterBible.org look up the Greek or Hebrew word and definition of one of those words.

Write your findings below.

[ ] Write down any general thoughts or questions you have as you read the passage.

Treasured and Pondered: Day Three

Declaration Verse: Luke 2:19

Today's Declare Practice: Imagine

[ ] Read Luke 2:19

Insert yourself in the story as you ponder the following questions. Use your imagination and all your senses to be present in the scene.

[ ] When and where is this taking place? **What do you imagine you might see, hear, touch, taste, or smell?**

[ ] Who is speaking or writing? Whom are they addressing? Others? God? Themselves?

[ ] What are they speaking or writing about? What is their purpose?

Have a little more time?

[ ] What character traits of God are shown through the Declaration Verse?

   Is He steadfast, faithful, just, trustworthy, nurturing, kind, gentle, or strong?
   What do you see revealed about His nature in this passage of Scripture?

[ ] What promises of God are shown through the Declaration Verse?

   Write any observations, key words, or questions you have as you ponder the
   Declaration Verse. If you have time, you may want to do another word study.

Digging Deeper
Galatians 4:4-7

[ ] Imagine

You may want flip back to the beginning of Galatians in your Bible to read the introduction or use on online resource. Paul wrote this letter to the church around A.D. 49, just a few years after Mary's death.

Imagine you are there when Paul's letter is being read to the church in Galatia. What do you notice? How might Christ followers react to these words?

[ ] Write down any general thoughts or questions you have as you read the verses.

Treasured and Pondered: Day Four

Declaration Verse: Luke 2:19

Today's Declare Practice: Listen

> *Remember to take a moment to Engage as you prepare to listen: toss, catch, invite, open, expect. Invite the Words of Scripture and the Words of God to speak personally into your mind and heart. Remember that God's voice will never accuse you. He may bring gentle conviction, and that can cause some grief, but God always brings hope.*

Listening can be pursued for several days, and in fact, God will probably speak unexpectedly at random times of day or night as His revelation is released to you. Ask these questions as you listen to God's voice:

[ ] How do these verses apply to me?

Have a little more time?

[ ] Ponder and pray: how I can apply these truths to the frustrations, disappointments, fears, or hurts in my life? Is there anything I need to receive or surrender in my life?

Digging Deeper
Galatians 4:4-7

[ ] Listen

   Ask yourself: how does Galatians 4:4-7 apply to me? What does God want to speak to my heart through this story?

[ ] Write down any general thoughts or questions you have as you read the verses.

Treasured and Pondered: Day Five

Declaration Verse: Luke 2:19

Today's Declare Practice: Declare

Write out a declaration of what you have received as you meditated on the Word. This can be a statement of God's promise to you, an affirmation of the healing that He has given you, or a proclamation of a truth that has become real to you. A declaration can include Scripture, your own words, or some of each.

Reflect upon your week

Write out Luke 2:19 by hand if you memorized it or summarize the Declaration Verse in your own words below.

Spend a few minutes documenting your insights, "a-ha" moments, and revelations from this week of digging into the Bible.

Digging Deeper
Galatians 4:4-7

[ ] Write any notes or observations you made from the verses you read.
   Is there one verse that stands out to you?

[ ] Did you have any new insights as you pondered this passage this week?

Week Four: Discussion Topics

Use these discussion topics to gather with friends and enjoy this study together. You are welcome to use these points to help guide your conversation, or you can ponder these questions as a personal reflection. Even if you are not able to meet up with a girlfriend, you're invited to join us in our private Facebook Group at facebook.com/groups/flourishgathering/

1) Do you have any thoughts or reactions to this week's devotional? We have included two passages that may inspire an interesting conversation:

> *"When we fail to remember the promises, we gradually drift from His way. If our gaze is not fixed daily on God, our eyes wander to distractions, and before long we find ourselves on other paths, confused about our direction, unsure where we are on the map . . . or maybe we have lost the map altogether, and we find ourselves chasing lesser things." (page 85)*

> *"Growth is accomplished in our lives quietly, gradually, incrementally, in the normal stuff of daily living. . . . Let us ponder all that He has done. I encourage you to allow God to take you on a reflective journey to find the treasure in your journey. Spend time with Mary as you discover your story of "Yes." (page 86)*

2) Was there a special insight you gained from the **Investigate** practice? Perhaps an interesting word study, cross reference, or commentary?

3) What happened when you used your **Imagination**? What did you discover about the context of this chapter or book of the Bible? If you had time, did you gain insight into the character or promises of God?

4) Did God speak something special that you would like to share as you **Listened**?
5) What is your **Declaration**? How can we pray for you in this regard?
6) How about the Ruth reading plan? Anything interesting there?
7) How can we support one another this week? Prayer requests? Praise reports?

Notes

Notes

Next Steps

What a joy it has been to journey with you during this season of your life. We trust that you have a new awe for Mary, the mother of Jesus our Lord. We marvel at her life yielded to God and her steadfast determination to make His Word her way, so rare in this time when selfishness is commonplace.

We delight in her faithfulness. Of her choosing, she confidently sets foot on a path that she knows will include both joy and heartache. She acquiesces to God, eyes wide open, aware of the prophesies about the difficult life promised to her son, the Messiah. Nevertheless, she chooses to be faithful to the call. She does not shrink back from the weighty honor that she has been called to bear.

We admire her desire to find shelter in the Word, away from the tumult of life, and to seek God in the quiet of her inner ponderings. She treasures the Words of Scripture, the words of Gabriel, and the promises of her faith. As Mary discovers the satisfaction of a life of obedience, she knows the reward of being treasured by her Father.

We trust that you have tasted of the depth and richness to be discovered in the DECLARE Bible Study Approach. One friend likens it to "Holy Spirit sunglasses" that allow you to see through the surface into the deep waters: "I've been able to see deeper into the Bible than I've ever done before. The Holy Spirit has used DECLARE to bring much more life into my Bible time." This sister is using DECLARE to study the book of Galatians with a friend. With regular use, it becomes your own personal tool to dig into any part of the Bible with an expectation of opening the Word and hearing God's voice.

May the seeds planted in your life grow and bloom as you cultivate a heart like Mary. Until we meet again, keep on Flourishing.

A Note to Group Leaders

We are pleased that you have chosen to gather a group of ladies to enjoy this Flourish Bible Study together. The study is designed to create deep, thoughtful conversations. Chatting through the insights gained using the five simple DECLARE practices each week will guide the discussion to reveal personal "a-ha's" that come straight from Scripture. It is motivating and encouraging when ladies share how God speaks in their lives.

We have provided here a few considerations regarding scheduling:
- Since it is a four-week study, you have several choices for your meeting schedule. You can meet up weekly for four weeks, or maybe you meet only twice and cover two weeks at a time. Most groups enjoy 1-1/2 or 2 hours together.
- Some groups like to add a fifth meeting time to gather before the study begins to hand out the books and view the first video. See below for suggestions in the use of the video resources.

The Flourish Experience resources have been created to enhance your gathering:
- The **Weekly Teaching Videos** provide approximately 15 minutes input from Jenny and Mindy.
- This weekly video can be shown at the beginning of your meeting time, or at the end. Alternatively, you can assign the video material for women to watch at home before they come.

We suggest that you make use of the weekly **Discussion Topics** located at the end of each week to facilitate the discussion. You may want to reserve fifteen minutes or so at the end of your group time to share prayer requests.

Gathering women to share their stories invites God's love to shine: *"They triumphed over him by the blood of the Lamb and by the word of their testimony." (Revelation 12:11)* We pray you are blessed as you flourish together!

A little bit about Flourish

Flourish is a gathering of women who passionately pursue God and His Word. We encourage one another through genuine, transparent relationships which equip us to thrive where we are planted and impact our world for the glory of God.

We believe that the power of God's Word revealed by the Spirit changes lives. In relationship with God and with one another, we are strengthened to overcome hindrances in our journey. Flourish is dedicated to bringing God's Word to life in the 21st Century by encouraging women that the Word is alive, active, and powerful today.

Now here's our purpose spelled out in regular talk.

We want more of God, so we dig into His Word. We can't survive without Him. We can't survive without you either. You can leave your mask at the door because real life is messy, and no one here is pretending to have it all together

At Flourish we...

ENCOURAGE

We share real stories of real life with transparency and honesty, always pointing to the promises found in God's Word.

EQUIP

Flourish provides tools and resources that are grounded in the Word of God. Our community provides a safe place to learn and to grow.

ACTIVATE

We seek God in community because, when the rubber hits the road, we want to see evidence of God's life in our relationships.

About the Authors

Meet Mindy . .

Mindy Kiker is a committed Floridian, enjoying a quiet woodland home that she and her husband built to shelter their four boisterous boys. Born in Tucson, Arizona, Mindy's magical childhood included a four-year hiatus on the big island of Hawaii where she danced the hula, and later helped with the family marina in Cedar Key where she learned to cast net and sail the Gulf of Mexico. The Kikers spent the 1990s in South Africa, returning with their brood for a sabbatical year in 2012 to reconnect with beloved friends and favorite places.

Now that Mindy's spring-chicken days are drawing to a close, she has accepted her role as an "older" woman (it's all relative) cheering others on in life's journey. A favorite verse that motivates her to keep pressing into God and encouraging her friends to do the same is *Galatians 5:1, "It is for freedom that Christ has set us free. Stand firm, then, and do not let yourselves be burdened again by a yoke of slavery."*

And Jenny. . .

Jenny Kochert was born and raised in sunny South Florida. Although she took full advantage of big-city life growing up, she longed to move to a quieter town, and college provided the perfect excuse! After graduating from the University of Florida, Jenny followed in the family footsteps and became a private investigator (yes, you read that right!), opening her own agency in 2005.

However, once she became a mom to her daughter, Sophia, she turned in her badge, and settled at home, now home schooling her daughter. Jenny, her husband Ryan, and daughter Sophia now live in Northern Kentucky where they serve in ministry together as a family. God has put a story on her lips and a passion in her heart to encourage women, and she is thrilled that she gets to do that each and every day.

Thank you

for joining us!

Connect with us on Facebook:

@Flourishgathering

Contact us:

info@flourishgathering.com

Visit us:

Flourishgathering.com

Made in the USA
Lexington, KY
14 November 2018